Dogs

Boxers

by Jody Sullivan Rake

Consulting Editor: Gail Saunders-Smith, PhD

Consultant: Jennifer Zablotny, DVM
Member, American Veterinary Medical Association

Capstone press
Mankato, Minnesota

Pebble Books are published by Capstone Press,
151 Good Counsel Drive, P.O. Box 669, Mankato, Minnesota 56002.
www.capstonepress.com

1 2 3 4 5 6 12 11 10 09 08 07

Library of Congress Cataloging-in-Publication Data
Rake, Jody Sullivan.
    Boxers / by Jody Sullivan Rake.
    p. cm.—(Pebble Books. Dogs)
    Summary: "Simple text and photographs present an introduction to the boxer
breed, its growth from puppy to adult, and pet care information"—Provided
by publisher.
    Includes bibliographical references and index.
    ISBN-13: 978-1-4296-0809-1 (hardcover)
    ISBN-10: 1-4296-0809-9 (hardcover)
    1. Boxer (Dog breed)—Juvenile literature. I. Title. II. Series.
SF429.B75R35 2008
636.73—dc22   2007000895

Note to Parents and Teachers

The Dogs set supports national science standards related to life
science. This book describes and illustrates boxers. The images
support early readers in understanding the text. The repetition of
words and phrases helps early readers learn new words. This book
also introduces early readers to subject-specific vocabulary words,
which are defined in the Glossary section. Early readers may need
assistance to read some words and to use the Table of Contents,
Glossary, Read More, Internet Sites, and Index sections of the book.

Table of Contents

Loving Boxers

Boxers enjoy being
around kids.
They love spending time
with their families.

Brave boxers will stand between a family member and a stranger.

From Puppy to Adult

Five to ten boxer puppies are born in each litter. Boxer puppies are playful.

Boxer puppies are friendly to people they know.

Adult boxers are
medium-sized dogs.
They are a little taller
than a doll house.

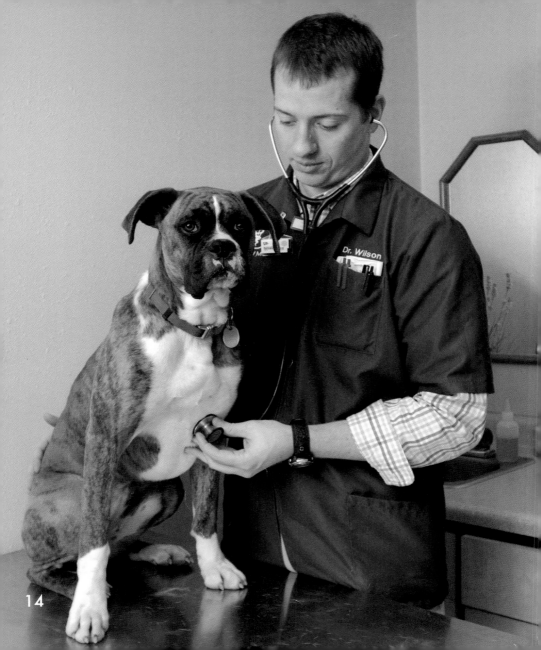

Taking Care of Boxers

Boxers need food and water every day. Regular visits to the vet keep them healthy.

Boxers lick themselves
like cats do.
Their short hair
only needs to be brushed
once a week.

Boxers need exercise.
Owners should walk
their boxers twice a day.

Brave boxers make good watchdogs and loving pets.

Glossary

brave—willing to do hard things

friendly—helpful and kind

healthy—fit and well, not sick

litter—a group of animals born at one time to the same mother

playful—full of energy

vet—a doctor that takes care of animals

watchdog—a dog trained to guard a house, property, or people

Read More

Bozzo, Linda. *My First Dog.* My First Pet Library from the American Humane Association. Berkeley Heights, N.J.: Enslow, 2007.

Einhorn, Kama. *My First Book about Dogs.* Sesame Subjects. New York: Random House, 2006.

Internet Sites

FactHound offers a safe, fun way to find Internet sites related to this book. All of the sites on FactHound have been researched by our staff.

Here's how:

1. Visit *www.facthound.com*

2. Choose your grade level.

3. Type in this book ID **1429608099** for age-appropriate sites. You may also browse subjects by clicking on letters, or by clicking on pictures and words.

4. Click on the **Fetch It** button.

FactHound will fetch the best sites for you!

23

Index

Word Count: 109
Grade: 1
Early-Intervention Level: 14

Editorial Credits
Becky Viaene, editor; Juliette Peters, set designer; Kim Brown, book designer;
Kara Birr, photo researcher; Karon Dubke, photographer; Kelly Garvin, photo stylist

Photo Credits
BigStockPhoto.com/joeygil, 18; Capstone Press/Karon Dubke, 4, 6, 12, 14, 16, 20;
Mark Raycroft, cover, 1, 10; Ron Kimball Stock/Ron Kimball, 8

Capstone Press thanks the Minnesota Valley Pet Hospital in Mankato, Minnesota for their
assistance with this book.